AF316655

# GONEFISHING INDIA

# GONEFISHING INDIA

SUPRIO MUKHERJEE

# Notion Press

Old No. 38, New No. 6
McNichols Road, Chetpet
Chennai - 600 031

First Published by Notion Press 2017
Copyright © Suprio Mukherjee 2017
All Rights Reserved.

ISBN

Paperback  978-1-948147-70-5

Hardcase  979-8-89519-227-6

# ACKNOWLEDGEMENTS

My uncles, Prashanta, Prabir Ganguly and Jayanta Banerjee, not only provided me with my initial tackle but also let me accompany them on their fishing trips. My grandmother Urmila Ganguly was my greatest 'protector' during those early years. I miss her more than words can express.

Kalida, who frowned upon anything heavier than a 6 lb line for Carp and helped me understand ground bait and hook bait.

My lifelong friend, fishing mate and mentor, Vinay Badola, without whom this book would not have existed.

Alam, Sidhaiya, Dileep, Kanta and the other boys who taught me so much.

Darran Davis and the entire team of Aquacreed.

# CHAPTER 1

I could hear the sound of rain! Monsoon rain!

Somewhere from a distance, someone called, checking for me.

The "Batas" (*Labeo Bata)* were in a feeding frenzy, and my bucket already held over a score and a few Carp brats. The water was dark and deep. A few big Carps were feeding near the lily pod. It had started raining heavily, drowning all other sounds except the drumming of raindrops on the umbrella. Even the oversized umbrella was grossly inadequate in keeping the raindrops away, and I was already soaked to the skin, but I knew a couple of big Carps were still lurking below, waiting for a chance to snack on the juicy earthworm dangling from the hook, and I was not about to run for shelter.

And then, a big Rohu took the bait and bent the pole like a bow. I was struggling to keep a hold of my rod, but the fish was winning. It was battle royal, and I was being pulled into the water. I woke up with a start, transported many decades forward. Thankfully, it was a Saturday, and I could afford to indulge in a little more of "fishing" without getting out of bed.

I grew up in an estate in the suburb of what was then Calcutta, where I waited for my grandfather and uncles to leave for office and then take out my most treasured possession, a five-foot bamboo pole with fine "moonga silk" line, an inch of peacock quill float, the smallest hook, possibly size 18, with a lead weight, couple of inches above the hook.

With a small ball of atta dough, some earthworms – freshly dug out and wrapped in a piece of banana leaf – and a small bucket to keep the fish, I was all set to conquer the world. The short walk to the chosen pond or tank was covered in the quickest possible time. With the spot for the day chosen, I settled down for the next couple of hours. I had more fun when it rained. I loved rain. It was like being in my own private world – the smell, the feel; everything appeared freshly washed. And after the rain stopped, I enjoyed nature's symphony! Overhead, a flock of parrots flew by, calling, crows flapped their wet wings, trying to dry themselves as best as possible, and the frogs croaked. From overhanging branches, drops of rainwater plopped into the pond, sending off tiny ripples in concentric circles. Patches of freshly washed blue sky wrapped in whiffs of white clouds smiled indulgently. The dragonflies were out, flitting from leaf to leaf of the water plants, which trembled in the mild moisture-laden breeze. My bucket, half-filled with water, filled up with Poonti (Rosy Barb), Bata and Carp brats. A couple of hours and I had 25 to 30 fish in the bucket.

Sometimes, my grandmother joined in. Everyone fished at home, but I always preferred to fish alone. Grandmother, I did not mind, but others made small talk and laughed loudly. I preferred solitude in order to catch the biggest fish in the world or stalk that man-eater in the Himalayan foothills, which had already killed over 100 people. That was my world!

I was on that magical mystery tour.

# CHAPTER 2

It was a lazy October day. The sun shone bright and crisp, but the ferocity of summer was gone, replaced by a soft warm glow of early winter. I was out fishing with my two uncles on a lake. Actually, they were fishing, and I was around. I was always around when someone was fishing. There were always a thousand things to be done, and I guess people were glad to get some help and would bear my presence.

My younger uncle chose a spot under a huge jamun tree, and the elder uncle decided to cast from a head jutting out into the water. The choice and selection of your spot for the day is a fascinating task. Years of being at the water's edge and then one's own gut feel goes into deciding which areas are likely to yield results. Years of Carp fishing gave me some understanding of reading the water, and it is a pleasurable activity even when you are not carrying a rod.

As this was a private lake, there was nobody else in sight. The ground bait was soon ready and into the water some 15–20 feet away. The durrie was spread out, the rods were readied, and the hook was baited. Bread paste was kneaded together with all the other masalas that the Carp anglers had put together. The formulations and proportions were guarded zealously. The rest of the hook bait was stored in an airtight container to be used for the rest of the day. One by one, all three lines were cast, and the rods were secured in the rod holders. Then, the wait began.

On the far side, I could see my younger uncle reeling in some decent-sized Rohus. We had also started to get a few nibbles and line bites. Suddenly, one of the floats started bobbing in a mad dance and *whoosh* – it disappeared below the surface, and the centre pin reel started to sing. Fish on! The two-piece pale blue fibreglass rod had a nice bend. About 30–40 metres of 8 lb monofilament line had peeled off effortlessly when my uncle handed over the rod to me. A huge flock of butterflies were flapping mightily in my stomach, and my heart was pounding so violently that I was sure everyone could hear it. I took the rod. The fish must have realised that it was a heaven-sent opportunity to break free and made a dash for a bed of floating water hyacinth on the far side.

Now, the problem with the centre pin reels is that there is no drag, and one has to use one's thumb to slow the fish down. At a ripe old age of 8 years, one was still to learn these tricks of the trade.

After a while, the fish slowed down, and I started to reel him in. It seemed like ages when I tried to bring in the biggest fish of my life. My younger uncle had by then kept his rod aside, and he came to help me land my first fish with rod and reel.

The fish, sensing the commotion on the bank, made another mad dash but stayed clear of any snag. Inch by inch, I gained line, and then the fish came into view.

The landing net was out, and gradually, a tired 3 kg Catla was guided into the net.

The pat on the back is still a vivid memory.

# CHAPTER 3

For a major part of my life, I have been a Carp angler. Lakes, ponds, tanks and dams had plenty of large-sized Carps to keep the occasional angler more than interested. In and around Calcutta, there were some great fishing spots: day ticket lakes, private tanks and ponds and marshy land for snakeheads. Most Sundays, unless otherwise scheduled, were always fishing days. That weekend, we were set to fish in one of the private lakes located some thirty odd miles away in a village. The flurry of activities preceding Carp fishing starts building up a few days before the actual fishing day/s, reaching a feverish pitch by the time one reaches the water's edge.

The previous few days were spent in getting ground and hook bait ready. An entire volume of bait encyclopaedia can be put together describing the variety of ground bait that I am aware of, and every self-respecting Carp angler has a similar sized encyclopaedia stored in his memory.

And then, there are hook baits...

Next morning, we reached the lake at about 8.00 hours. It was a beautiful 10-odd acre lake with an island in the middle. There was an old temple in ruin with trees and creepers all over the brickwork. The lake was clean, and the water was deep and dark. I tested the depth before ground baiting. There were overhanging branches from some really old mango trees providing shade from the blazing sun, a couple of cormorants were busy fishing, a common kingfisher was keeping vigil, and a light breeze was forming ripples in the water. I could see some big Carps move towards my left between lily pods.

I got three rods ready and made the bread paste hook bait with all the additives and lapped with ant eggs, locally known as *tipi*. Once all three rods were in the water, I checked the time – 8.25 hours!

Within the next half an hour, I could see the presence of fish in the swim. At such times, the body goes taut, lips and throat dry up in anticipation, and imagination plays games with the mind. However, since I got into catch and release, I am much more relaxed, as the fear of losing a fish is gone. I guess I am a better angler for that.

Soon, the float started to quiver and then was bobbing ever so gently. This gentle dance went on for about a quarter of an hour and then *WHOOSH!* The float went under. HIT! The reel started singing as the line started to peel off. Fish on! After about 50 yards of mad rush, the fish turned left, towards the island. I could see branches from sunken trees sticking out, and the lily pod was not too far away. There were too many snags to handle with an 8 lb line. As the fish was still moving rapidly, I dropped the rod towards the right, which had the desired effect – the fish turned. The next 15 odd minutes saw the fish being reeled into about 5 metres of the shore and then again make a run for it. At such times, it is critically important to keep the drag loose. This happened a couple of times till the fish moved into some tall and very dense grass growing in the shallows towards my right. Then all movement stopped. The fish must have tangled the line and gotten away. Cursing at my luck, I tried to reel in the line, but it was stuck. Now I had to get into the water to untangle my line. Gingerly, I stepped into the water and tried to locate the snag. Suddenly, I could see the fish, reddish-orange fins and tail, torpedo-like shape, resting on the grass bed.

Ever so gently I freed the line, and now the line from the fish was directly in touch with the rod tip. Cradling the rod in my left arm and the landing net in my right, I tried to close in, but by now the fish was well rested and regained its strength. Seeing the landing net, the fish jerked free off the grass bed and made a dash for open water, in the process nearly yanking the rod out of my left hand.

Casting aside the landing net, I somehow managed to keep hold of the rod. Standing in waist-deep water, surrounded by tall grass and a feisty Rohu peeling off the line, the odds were stacked against me. I somehow scrambled back to dry land and moved back in order to keep the fish away from the grass bed.

Gradually, I gained line again and after a couple of short runs, I guided the fish into the waiting landing net. It was a beautiful 15+ lb Rohu, red and orange intermingled with the silver. It was not until a decade and a half later that I was onto catch and release, so this one went straight into the keep net.

It was a very good beginning to the day.

# CHAPTER 4

A mild jerk and the train came to a halt. I saw the time on my cell phone; it was 5.00 am. One backpack, the camera bag and the rod tube slung from my shoulder did not make climbing down to the low platform easy.

A few light bulbs were flickering against the backdrop of an ink blue sky. The quaint, sleepy railway station was wet from the previous night's rain. There was an early morning chill in the air, typical of the Himalayan foothills. I made my way through a few cab drivers trying to grab their next fare, to find Balamda, who was supposed to meet me at the 'station' and was going to drive me to camp. A cheerful shake of the hand, bags stowed away at the back of the olive green painted Gypsy, and we were off but not before a reviving, refreshing cup of very sweet, thick tea. As soon as we drove out of town and into the open, the piercing chilly wind took over the open Gypsy. A half hour later, we were knocking on Vinay's door. A long-time fishing mate, Vinay was arguably the very best I have fished with. A treasure trove of knowledge and a heart of gold, no one could ever wish for more. One bear hug later, Vinay's belongings finding space at the rear, we were off again. Conversation is difficult in an open vehicle, but this was alright with us since we had a week together to catch up. The drive was spectacular, to say the least.

The Corbett Tiger Reserve lies to your left and the Kosi River to your right. There is always a chance to get some wildlife sightings – chital, wild boar, barking deer and who knows, maybe a leopard or even Royalty himself. However, we had no such luck that day, and an hour later, with 4 WD in operation, we scampered up the last steep stretch into the camp. The camp dogs gave a welcome bark; the camp was already waking up. It was a homecoming of sorts.

A couple of cups of tea allowed us to catch up with the happenings of the past few months. E-mails and periodic long distance phone calls are a poor substitute for hardcore *adda*. Facebook was yet to be born.

The sun was out, and tiny droplets from the previous night's rain nestled on the leaves, sparkling like a million tiny diamonds. The birdlife in the sub-Himalayan landscape is awesome, and a hearty breakfast, accompanied by this glorious symphony is what makes life worth living, and life takes on a different hue after a good meal!

More chai, organising the gear for the day, packing lunch, water, tea in flasks, everything into the Gypsy, and we were off to spend the day next to the most beautiful river.

Quarter of an hour later, we got the first glimpse of the river glistening in the morning sun. The water was slightly muddy because of the previous night's rain, but we knew it would clear up soon. We would get different water conditions ranging from muddy to gin clear over the next few days. Soon we had to leave the main road and drive down the unpaved village track towards the river. Once the car stopped, nature's music took over – the sound of the river and chirping birds. Despite having spent so many years in these surroundings, the intense happiness of just being there never diminishes.

We had to cross the river by a footbridge and walk downriver to reach our favourite pool from where we would start casting and then gradually travel downstream.

From under the bridge, the river travels another half a mile before plunging down a long rapid. Then the river flows down for another half a mile into a deep dark pool and then down a steep rapid downstream. We had had some wonderful battles with the majestic Golden Mahseer in these waters, and I was looking forward to a great day's angling.

The grass was still wet. Walking down steep slopes and then climbing up with all the fishing gear needs getting used to. The sand sticks to your shoes, and if you are not wearing socks, it gets into your shoes and bruises your feet.

The river had started clearing and was light brownish in colour. Once we reached the pool, I got my rod ready. An eight-foot spinning rod with a spinning reel loaded with 12 lb monofilament line joined with 15 lb fluorocarbon leader with a 90 lb test swivel. I put a few spinners, plugs and spoons in my pocket, and we spread out. I started casting a plug above the rapid. I usually 'spin' with a tightish drag when casting anywhere above a rapid for if the fish decides to go downstream, then there is no way that I will be able to land her. The third cast had a take – fish on...

This one was a Tor Putitora brat of about 10 lb but put up a brave fight, using the current to its advantage. Some 10 minutes later, we were releasing the fish, watching it swim away – always a glorious sight.

Meanwhile, downstream, Vinay was onto something much bigger – the fish went upstream against the current and then dashed off downstream, and then, suddenly, the line went limp. The fish was on for less than a minute, and when the terminal tackle came back, crumpled, we knew it was a Red Fin Mahseer. The Red Fins have tremendously powerful lips and can 'chew' and destroy the best hooks. Once, while holding up a 20 lb Red Fin for a photo, the fish gently closed its lip, and my right thumb bore the brunt of the vice-like lip strength. The pain lasted for well over a fortnight.

We had a couple more fish but all below 15 lb. It was around midday, and the sun was overhead. Lures were not being so effective now so we decided to take the bait rods out, catch some Chilwa as live bait and see if we could get something big. As Alam went to snag some Chilwas, we sat in the shade and poured ourselves some tea and got the bait rods ready.

Alam returned some half an hour later with some 8–10 Chilwas in a plastic bottle, hook caught upstream where a narrow stream joined the main river. Soon we had two bait rods out. In these mountain rivers, we tie a small stone from the swivel as weight, which keeps the baitfish free and swimming and the line submerged.

We had the first take around half an hour later. The reel started singing, and the fish had taken out some 40–50 yards of line in no time. With improvements in tackle, light and strong carbon fibre rods, improved drag in reels, lines, etc., and coupled with lower and lower water levels, one rarely gets those 100–200 metre runs, which Corbett sahib describes in his stories. This one put up a good fight though, but I was able to stop him well short of the rapid. Inch by inch, the line was retrieved. Twice, the fish went around some boulders, but the line held. Two shorter runs and we were unhooking a beautiful Golden of 30 lb. Some quick photographs and the fish was walked to slightly deeper waters to be revived. Holding the fish facing upstream and letting the oxygen-rich water flow through the gills, I could feel the fish regain its strength. Releasing a wild fish and seeing it swim away gracefully is one of the most amazing sights, and it makes this sport really worth it.

We had a couple more fish on bait – nothing spectacular but enough to keep our spirits up.

We sat under the shade of an oak tree to have a simple lunch of sandwiches washed down with lukewarm tea.

The sun had by now lost its intensity, and Vinay had his fly rod out. I was busy spinning with various lures and landing some nice Goldens, but hearing the commotion downstream, I knew Vinay was onto something big. As I turned the corner, I could see a nice bend on Vinay's fly rod and a lot of action – running up and down and shouting. As I went closer, I could see the fin and tail sticking out of the water. It was definitely a 20 + lb fish on fly. The fish made two more runs, and by the time the fish was landed, unhooked, revived and released, it was getting dark. We still had some walking to do through tiger country, to get back to the waiting car.

What a wonderful day by the river!

# CHAPTER 5

The climb down to the river from the road took over a quarter of an hour. A few jungle fowls, feeding under the early morning sun, hurriedly moved away from the winding mountain path to the thick adjoining undergrowth. The dry leaves, now moisture laden, soft and wet from overnight dew, made climbing down the steep mountain path called Pakdandi, that much more slippery.

A seasonal stream joins the river at this point and forms a confluence, Sangam, from where the river flows a further 200 metres, narrowing down gradually, before plunging through a boulder-strewn rapid.

The water was a bit cold, slightly coloured from the rains in the upper reaches, and the morning air was crisp. It was about 7 am; the sun had risen about half an hour back.

A couple of casts across the Sangam yielded no results, not even a follow, so I had a long cast across the river and allowed the current to carry the silver spoon downstream. The line was flowing out. I closed the bail arm and started to retrieve and immediately had a 'take' and felt the weight of the fish. I saw the line tighten and felt the pressure. FISH ON! Now the line was peeling off, and I knew I had a fight on my hands.

The fish made off towards the rapid and had already started using the current to its advantage. He had already taken out about 70–80 metres of line, and I had a task at hand to fight the fish back up the river or out of the current. There was no way I could follow the fish downstream, as there was a rocky wall some 15 metres downstream, and this little gravelly slope was the only piece of flat land from where I could safely fight and land the fish.

I would gain about two metres of line and then lose five. The fish was playing me, using the current to its full advantage. After what seemed like eternity, I realised that I had lost more line than I had gained. It was a stand-off and possibly the fish was marginally ahead in round one. My forearm was sore.

Then the fish decided to change his strategy and started sulking, and I was not able to budge him an inch. I tightened the drag slightly and applied more pressure. The 15 lb line was taut, glistening in the morning sun as beads of water slid off it and then when the rod had a proper bend and the line was really taut, I opened the bail arm, and the fish was dislodged from its position behind the boulder and swept away by the current. I quickly closed the bail arm, dropped the rod towards my left and started winding. The fish now did not have the help of the current to fight me, but he was a decent-sized fish, and his bulk made it a task to reel him in. Inch by inch, foot by foot, I was getting him to move upstream. As he came closer, I could see his red fin and tail sticking out of the water surface.

As he came closer, I loosened the drag a bit, as I knew he would make at least one more run, and I was concerned about the health of the line. Soon, he was on his second run, and this time, he took out about 40–50 metres of line. This time, I was careful in keeping him away from the main channel, so fighting him back was easier. However, I was fighting the fish on a loose drag, as I was afraid that the main line and the fluorocarbon leader might have gotten frayed when the fish was behind the boulder, sulking. Sulking is when the fish puts its head down and opens its fins, making it virtually impossible to dislodge him.

There was a short third run, but now the fish was ready for landing. The landing mat was out, and soon I was guiding a beautiful Red Fin Mahseer into the landing net.

Unhooking the fish, taking a couple of pictures and holding the fish facing upstream to revive it were completed in the quickest possible time.

Watching the beautiful animal swim away was and will always be a pleasure.

# CHAPTER 6

I had a couple of days off and what better way to spend it than to take off for a short trip to the river of my dreams! Starting well before sunrise and driving through the familiar route, I reached the outskirts of the Corbett Tiger Reserve where I was to rendezvous with Vinay. A quick lunch and we reached the resort on the banks of the Ramganga River where Alam was waiting for us.

I was keen to go out spinning immediately, so setting up my rod did not take too much time. The river is a short walk from the resort, and soon I was casting into the muddy June water. The next couple of hours were spent landing and releasing brat-sized Mahseer, and when the sun disappeared behind the mountains, it was time to trek back. The evening was warm, humid, and post-dinner, there was a sharp shower that brought some relief.

Next morning, we set out with some bait rods along with spinning rods. The water had cleared up a bit; that meant that there was not much rain in the upper reaches of the river. Spinning with a variety of lures was fun, and we had a couple of fish over 10 lb. Soon, the sun was beating down from the clear blue sky, and we rigged up the bait rods. Two of the lines were cast with live bait and one with atta, and then we sat down in the shade of some rocks to wait.

The first take was a beauty – the rod tip quivered then bent over, and the reel started to scream. As I picked up the rod, all went quiet. At such moments you get frustrated, angry, especially when you realise that the fish was lost due to a faulty knot. You want to scream, punch and kick something (someone?). However, with two of the best fishing partners around to calm you down, the rod was re-jigged and cast again quickly enough.

The next fish was a beautiful black Mahseer, slightly over 15 lb that put up a valiant fight. Soon we had our second fish, well over 30 lb that took the atta bait! Three takes and 2 fish landed within the first couple of hours;

not bad at all. The pain of losing the first wish was somewhat numbed.

Alam had climbed up to the road to try and organise some tea, when the third rod, rigged with a half lb Carp, started to bend over. By the time I was able to pick up the rod and engage the bait runner, the fish had taken out line and was rapidly moving towards the head of the rapid. This was a 10' rod, and the reel was loaded with 30 lb monofilament line, but if the fish went down the rapid, then I would lose it. Dropping the rod to my right, I was able to turn the fish somewhat and was gradually able to slow it down. The challenge of retrieving line with a leviathan attached to the other end against the current is an adrenalin-pumping challenge that anglers relish; however, a couple of other factors made the task even more challenging. I had not really noticed when the blue sky had been covered by rain-bearing dark clouds till it started to rain, accompanied by some thunder and lightning. Now, carbon fibre rods are good conductors of electricity, and I was not really enjoying the prospect of holding a 10' fishing rod with a stubborn fish attached to the other side, with flashes of thunder and blinding rain.

Thankfully, after a short furious spell, the rain began to let up, and the tired fish too was laid out on the landing mat. The fish tipped the scale at 45 lb and was soon revived and released.

We were all soaked to the skin, and with the sky threatening to open up once more, we decided to return. We had 3 Carps as bait, so we decided to keep them submerged in the water, and to keep the otters from enjoying some freebies, we tied some white polythene bags to a stick and planted it there.

The afternoon was a complete wash out with intermittent heavy showers, so after lunch, we sat on the verandah, watching the rain and the river and having endless cups of tea. And then some hours later it got dark, and the rain let up. The stars appeared one by one. In the gathering darkness, you could hear the river but not really see it.

Next morning, we made our way to the spot where the bait had been 'securely' hidden away only to realise that a few fluttering plastic bags were not a deterrent to otters. Here we were, with some bait rods and no bait. Vinay suggested that I float down a ball of atta without any weight attached and let the current carry it onwards. I changed the setup of my rod, removed the swivel and the leader, tied a single 3/0 hook directly to the mainline and cast a decent ball of atta into the rapid. About 10–15 metres of line had gone out, and a decent-sized fish turned at the base of the rapid. I had just finished telling Vinay that I wished this one took the bait when suddenly the reel started screaming.

Out of the thousands of fish I have landed, a few are permanently etched in my memory – each turn, each run, every movement. As I was fishing with free-floating atta on a light drag, the first run was really spectacular, possibly the longest I have seen in fresh water. The reel was loaded with about 150 metres of 12 lb line, and I could see the rapidly emptying spool. After about 100 metres or so, the fish stopped and then the line went limp. All kind of thoughts clouded the mind: *the line must have snapped, or maybe the knot was again fouled up or did the fish spit the hook?* I was winding the line when I felt that the line was stuck, snagged? This could mean only one thing – the fish had spat the hook out. Out of sheer frustration of first having lost the fish and then having got snagged, I kept on winding, caring little if the hook broke or the knot gave way when suddenly I felt movement, and line started going out. The fish was still on... After the first run, when the fish had stopped, it came upstream and must have come up fast, and I must have presumed it to be a lost fish. Now the fight was on again. The fish was now fighting a tighter drag and was on its second run. However, she was able to take out another 50–60 metres of line. This time, bringing her upstream was challenging. Pumping and winding gingerly, the line holding strong, the fish was brought to the tail of the rapid. Now the challenge was to bring the fish further up the rapid, as there was no way I could go further down the river, as there was a sheer rock wall blocking any route downstream. Trying to figure out what to do next gave the fish enough time to recover, and it took off on its third run. Using the force of the river, the fish took out a fair amount of line, and the hard work of gaining line and bringing the fish up had to be done all over again. The fish was now tired, and there was some slack water where the fish was guided to. Alam was waiting there, in waist-deep water, with the landing net.

Soon, we had the fish on the landing mat, and aching arms were finally getting some rest. It was a beautiful fish, well over 30 lb, glistening in the mid-morning sun. The fish was held facing upstream while the oxygen-rich river water revived her quickly.

What a fish!

# CHAPTER 7

The first sight of the river was breath-taking.

The overnight train crawled into the platform of the railway station of this bustling town in Central India. An open-top Gypsy was to take us to our destination some 60 km away.

A half hour later, when we had left the town behind, the rugged beauty of the landscape took over. There were bare mountains on one side and rolling land dotted with thorny bushes on the other.

The only sign of civilisation was the potholed metal road and HT cables visible intermittently.

When we drove through the gates of the rest house, and the car engine was switched off, I could hear the silence. Everything was so quiet except for the chirping of the birds. The rest house was a pre-Independence structure –large rooms with high ceilings and four-blade ceiling fans. I was in a different era.

Tea was served, hot, sweet and refreshing. Unpacking and a bath were followed by a simple lunch of rice and chicken curry. It was too hot to venture out even though it was only April; the afternoon sun was blazing hot. It was decided that we would go out only after 5.00 pm to have a look at the river.

The first sight of the river was breath-taking.

It really wasn't the river but the backwaters of the dam that seemed endless, like staring into the sea. Then beyond the sluice gates, the river flowed through rough, boulder-strewn channels and a sheer wall of rock on the far side. There were Magars and Gharials and gigantic Mahseers, Lanchi, Bowali and Catla that kept the big reptiles well fed. And the snakeheads were really something else! We could spot some huge fish swimming up and down the channel from the sluice gates to the pool below.

The countryside was bare with muscular rocks showing off their brute strength. Wild boars, deer, leopards and bears inhabited the hillocks and the wooded shrubs, which were visible, till the horizon where the sky merged into the hills. Once in a while, a tiger from the neighbouring reserve would stray into this mix and make things more interesting.

The men were primarily dressed in white with colourful safas and turbans. The women wore saris – red, yellow, green – as if to make up for the lack of colour nature had forgotten to splash! This was going to be our home for the next few days.

The sunset was spectacular; red and orange mingled together and changed colour every moment till stars began to appear one by one on the ink-blue backdrop. It was time to return to the rest house.

Dinner was simple, hot and tasty, and by 9.00 pm, we were ready to hit the sack.

Next morning, we left the rest house at around 6.00 am, drove down to the river's edge, made our way down and were soon casting amongst schools of Red Fin Mahseer. A couple of brats would follow the spoon but not take it. I cast beyond the schools and worked the lures into them, at varying speeds and depth – but nothing. I tried spinners too but with the same result. My local guide told me to be patient. *"8.00 baje jab pani chorega tab hoga."* Apparently, water would be released at 8.00 am, triggering a feeding frenzy.

So we waited. At exactly 8.00 am, a siren sounded, indicating that a sluice gate would open to release water. Then, gradually at first, and soon foaming, frothing water started to flow into the channel. We were about 250–300 metres downstream, casting away furiously. My local host had a take, about 40–50 metres of line was pulled out, and then all was quiet. This happened a second time to him so I went to check his setup and realised that the drag was too tight. I went up the channel and cast again and immediately had a take. The fish rushed upstream, then turned and went downstream. I had to be careful so that I was not snagged. In the gin-clear water, I could see the fish, and she was a beauty. I would bring her in, and then using the current, she would be off again. I moved downstream and gently eased her into the slack water after which landing her was just a matter of time. Despite strong opposition from my local hosts, the 20+ lb fish was unhooked, photographed and soon released.

One of my local hosts had a 10 lb fish, and I too reeled in 3 more fish of similar size. It was around 10.00 am and time for us to return. The strong sun was beating down, and I was glad to get into some shade.

Post lunch, we returned around 4.00 pm. This time we were taken to a spot further downstream for bait fishing. A local boatman who was drafted in to act as our ghillie soon had his cast net out and had got us enough live bait for the evening session. Three rods were rigged up and cast in the clear stretches amongst the boulders. It was extremely tricky, and mentally, I was trying to figure out a safe landing spot, when the rod farthest from me started to buckle. Quite a bit of the line had gone out when I clicked the bait runner into fighting drag. The fish had already gone around some boulders and had stopped. The water was not too deep, but I was reluctant to get into the water, as there were Magars in the river. Although there was no reported case of humans being attacked by crocs, I was not going to risk being the first. By this time, our ghillie had got his rickety country boat out, and following the line, had reached close to the fish. While his associate kept the boat in position, our ghillie carefully lifted the line and soon the rod tip was directly in touch with the fish.

The fish, now in open water and well rested, went upstream from where landing her was just a matter of time. This one was about 25 lb and was soon released. We had a Bowali (Wallago Attu) of about 15 lb that was harvested for dinner. By the time we made our way back to the rest house, the stars were out, and the blazing day had turned a little bit pleasant.

# CHAPTER 8

The southern break every December makes the Delhi winter more bearable. The December fishing at the Kaveri had become an annual pilgrimage, which was very pleasurable.

Leaving the chaotic Bangalore Airport with rod tubes and luggage was energy sapping, to put it mildly, but the Sunday traffic allowed us to get out of the city quickly enough. We made it to the fishing camp before sundown, stopping for lunch and coffee en route. Siddhaiya, ghillie unparalleled, was sought out, and latest fishing conditions were logged in. Siddhaiya doesn't speak a word of English or Hindi, and my knowledge of Kannada is conspicuous by its absence, yet every year, I only wanted to fish with him, and communication was never a problem.

A stroll down the sandy, rocky beach felt good. The warm evening breeze, the gorgeous Kaveri flowing ever so gently and then the music of the rapids from both upstream and down below the temple pool—life couldn't get better! No, actually, it could. The thought of hooking one of the Leviathans in these surroundings would be the ultimate joy.

The evening was spent unpacking the fishing gear and getting ready for an early morning departure.

My plan was to go upstream and cover all the pools over the next couple of days to assess the condition of the river. At the Kaveri, I prefer to use heavy rods, heavy reels with at least 50 lb line and 7/0 hooks. In any other Indian river, I would not use more than 25/30 lb line, but the razor-sharp rocks make Kaveri fishing a very different proposition altogether.

Over dinner, we met anglers from different parts of the world, who found Kaveri fishing enjoyable enough to return year after year. The conversation invariably centres on fishing updates since our last meeting.

I didn't need the alarm to wake me up at 6.00 am. Vinay was peacefully sleeping, but when coffee was ready, he was up in a flash. I checked the atmospheric pressure, and it was going to be a stable day. Over the last few years, I have started logging weather conditions like air temperature, water temperature and air pressure along with the catch and have some fantastic data.

We hit the water at 7.00. The sun was up, and the sky was shining bright and blue. Two rods were out, one with Chilwa and the other with ragi. We were soon into fish but not Mahaseer. The morning was spent reeling in the white Kaveri Catfish. We changed spots, changed pools, but the omnipresent Catfish were all around us. By 10.30 am, we decided to end the morning session.

The afternoon session was not much different, but I got a couple of Blue Fin Mahaseers under 10 lb and was back to the camp by 7.00 pm. The next day, we fished downriver, and it went very much like the previous day – lots of Catfish and some brat Mahaseers between 5–10 lb. On the third morning, I had a 15+ on ragi in a rapid on a light rod, and it fought like a tiger. There were some sharp jagged rocks sticking out of the water, which made the fight interesting, and the rapid added another dimension to it. More Catfish followed, and we were back for a late lunch.

I decided to fish the afternoon session from my favourite island near our camp. There were some small interesting islands formed by clusters of rocks jutting out, but this one had a small sandy beach also. Catfish and brat-sized Mahaseer kept us entertained, and then I enjoyed a beautiful sunset. Siddhaiya had thoughtfully packed a flask of hot tea, which was like an elixir. In the distance, I could hear the Dhols (wild dog) whistle their gathering call. In the jungle, very few animals dare tangle with the Dhol. They hunt down deer and antelopes by chasing them over long distances till the fatigued animal can go on no more.

One by one, the stars made their appearance. One could hear the river but in the gathering darkness, not see much. There are crocs in the river, but we had not heard of any encounter with humans. However, years spent in the wild has taught me to be cautious, so from the sandy beach I got back into the coracle and kept the rod on my side with my right hand resting on it. It was around 7.30 pm when the rod suddenly came to life. Like a bucking stallion, it reared up and went into a wild dance before I could get a grip on it. I hit once and then again. The darkness added a new variable. The fish felt nice and heavy. From the faint glow of light from the camp, I could make out the nice bend on my heavy rod. Line was peeling off, and the fish was using the fast flow of the channel to rush downriver. I knew that there were no rocks close by, but I was apprehensive about a few sunken logs to our left. Siddhaiya was excited and wanted to ensure that the drag was not overly tight. I had lost a big fish from the same spot the previous year, and he was determined that we land this one. Inch by inch, I gained on her, pumping ever so often and then she would start peeling off the heavy line again. This went on for about half an hour or so till her runs became shorter and shorter. A couple of short runs later, she was safely in Siddhaiya's arms. Weighing the fish in the dark between the two of us was a bit of a challenge, but it tipped the scale at over 40 lb.

Rowing back in the darkness was ever so pleasurable.

The next morning, we decided to fish downstream in one of the deepest pools in that stretch of the river. We left a little late and reached the pool at around 8.00 am. The sun was bright and the sky, pristine blue. The pool was dark and fairly still with weeds growing towards the far bank. The coracle was tied to one of those weed beds, and the line cast out with a decent-sized Chilwa. The depth of the pool could be gauged by the fact that the line settled nearly below the coracle at a depth of about 30 feet. I did not want to cast out the second rod, as I had a strange premonition that the second rod may come in the way and foul up the fight in case we were onto fish.

About a quarter of an hour had passed, when the rod tip started dipping and then went quiet. After a few moments, the same thing happened again. The third time, however, was different. The rod completely bent over, and the line started peeling off. Over 50 metres of line had gone out in no time, and the fish was showing no signs of slowing down. I tried to slow down the fast-emptying spool with my left palm, but the searing heat made that an impossible task. The only saving grace was that the pool was so deep that it had no snags to worry about as long as I could keep the fish under reasonable control. Gradually, the fish turned left but did not dive any deeper. Pumping ever so hard, I could only retrieve inches, but at least I had stopped the fish. Again and again, I kept on pumping; it was like lifting a boulder off the bottom of a well, a boulder with life. I didn't know how long this was going on or how long this was going to last. In the limited space of the coracle, I was cramped.

Gradually, I could feel the fish coming up, and soon I could see the dorsal fin and the tail. I could hardly believe the owner of those fins was attached to my line. Now the fish was visibly getting tired, and the pressure on the line was palpably reduced. The fish was now a few metres from the coracle, and expecting a second run, I loosened the drag on the reel a bit. As she came closer, the coracle and the rod spooked her, and she made another run, but the furious intensity was missing. She surfaced again and was soon lying on the wet landing mat laid at the base of the coracle for her.

We took the hook out and quickly completed our trophy photo session before lowering her down to the water and letting her revive in the pool. Soon, she was ready to go.

The size of the fish, its weight, length and girth, becomes immaterial over time. What stays with you is the memory of the fight in surreal surroundings – every moment, every movement, every twist and every turn. Everything gets etched in the memory forever.

# CHAPTER 9

Leaving behind the still-sleeping capital, we travelled through the green farmlands of western Uttar Pradesh, and for my French visitors, it was an intriguing journey. The sights, the food and the crowded Ghats of the rivers crossed were all a first-time experience for them. They wanted to capture the entire experience in as many photographs as they could. After Ramnagar, when we entered the forest area, they seemed to finally relax, and finally, after some 9 hours, for a journey, which I regularly cover in six and a half to seven hours, we reached the resort nestling amongst a mango grove on the banks of the Kosi River. In the evening, my guests decided to take a walk along the river. We had an early dinner and called it a day.

Next morning, we were up early. Soon, Alam, our guide, along with our local transport, arrived, and after a hearty breakfast and a couple of hours drive through the picturesque mountain road, we reached the road head where the next mode of transport – packhorses and mules – was waiting.

Loading the mules and mounting the horses, laughter and light banter notwithstanding, the party travelled down the Pakdandi, a narrow winding mountain trail for a couple of hours, disturbing Junglefowls, startling Chital and Barking Deer. In places, the Pakdandi was so narrow that one could see the steep drop right underneath, and it's fairly unnerving, to say the least. There was a village too that we passed on our way down, and our train of animals and people created quite a stir – excited dogs kept barking, curious children followed us till the end of the village and nonchalant cattle had to be goaded to make way, and we were off again.

Winding through the misty mountains – languid, glistening and shimmering – the first view of the river heightened our excitement. About half an hour later, we were easing our cramped bodies onto firm ground. A cool welcome drink later, it was time to quickly unpack and get the fishing gear set up. The typical Catfish setup is a heavy rod, 9–10' paired with a heavy bait runner reel loaded with 80 lb monofilament line. We used to use wire leader coated with monofilament earlier but have now switched to Kevlar, as the wire leader tends to damage the fish's lips. The hook used is 12/0 size, and the swivel for attaching the leader to the main line is 300–400 lb test. Setting up 2 rods took up some time, and the ever-alert boys, who arrived a day earlier, served lunch. Simple hot fresh food cooked with care and laid out under the shade of an old semal tree laden with flaming red flowers.

The short trek to the chosen pool for the day, over stones and boulders, could not have been covered quicker.

Two heavy rods with matching reels laden with half-pound Carps as bait were cast. Then the wait began.

Years of fishing in this river has given an insight into the behavioural pattern of these monsters. Goonch, the much maligned, mysterious Catfish, was the trophy we were seeking. Oodles of patience, staying power stamina and resolve are just not words: any angler hoping to hook one of these leviathans will realise that soon. The Goonch is a shy creature, and an opportunistic hunter will more often than not lie in wait for food to float down.

The pool is at the bottom of a small rapid with a white temple on the side of the hill in front. After the deep pool, the river flows through another half a mile, takes a sharp right turn and cascades down through a series of small rapids to a long deep pool with a beautiful sandy beach. Soon, we had a small group of curious boys returning from school for company. Fortunately, angling is not much of a spectator sport, and once the novelty factor had died down, the children disappeared. The field camp kept up a steady supply of flasks of coffee and biscuits. Gradually, the sun began to lose its intensity, and the sky turned inky blue, and stars began to appear. We made our way back to the camp.

Dinner again was a simple fare – hot, fresh and sumptuous.

The air mattress and sleeping bag in the two-man tent, although occupied by one person, is not the most comfortable but is no impediment to some sound sleep.

We woke up next morning to the sound of chirping birds and the smell of coffee. After a breakfast of fresh eggs, bread, fruit juice and more coffee, we hit the water real early. It was the beginning of another day full of hope and anticipation.

On the third evening, we landed our first fish – a 1.70 metre Goonch. The fish dashed off to the deepest part of the pool after having picked up the bait from the 'hole' at the tail of the rapid. Having reached the rocky shelves on the far side, the fish held fast. No amount of pumping, tightening and loosening of line could move the giant. Small stones were thrown to goad it into action but with little effect. After what seemed like an eternity, she moved, gently first and then a quick dash towards the shallow run-off. There, she paused and tried to return to the deep end, but the 80 lb monofilament line held firm and prevented the fish from doing so. Gradually, the fish came to the shallow water where the tail was quickly tied up and the fish secured. As this was a part of a documentary, the filming took some time. We also had a sharp drizzle while all this was going on, and finally, when the fish was released, she quickly dashed off towards the deep end of the pool. Mission successful, and the entire camp was in celebratory mode.

Next day, we decided to visit the local temple to pray and thank the lord for what we had already received. We had carried a couple of light-spinning rods and had some light tackle fun landing brat-sized Mahseer. We spent the afternoon visiting a local village and sampling some hot home-cooked local cuisine. When the birds started returning to their resting perches for the night, we made our way back to the camp.

A couple of days later, a 2.10-metre monster Goonch was landed from the same spot from where we had hooked the first one.

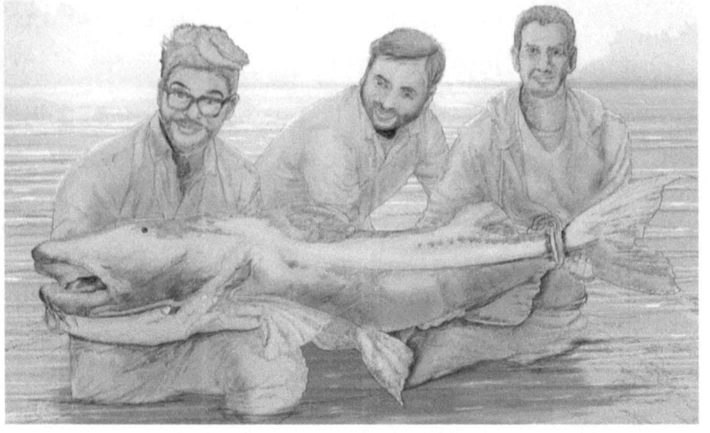

# CHAPTER 10

About a 3-hour drive away from Bangalore, including a breakfast break and time taken out to pick up some bait material and provisions, is the Forbes Sagar Lake, leased out to the Wildlife Association of South India (WASI). WASI has a couple of cottages on the banks of a smaller lake close to the Forbes Sagar. Close by, a British-era colony, replete with churches, a temple and a mosque, house the employees of the Shiva Samudram hydro electricity project. Some buildings of that era still stand, and it really is worth a visit.

Once a year, I visit the lake made famous by the Transworld Fishing Team, especially after the Cauvery fishing ban. The company of Sandeep Chakrabarti, an avid conservationist and an angler, is an added bonus.

Our usual routine is to wake up by 7.00 am, make some coffee and head out to the cottage lake with some ragi. After about an hour or so, go back to the cottage for breakfast. After washing up, head out again for a couple of hours to the cottage by the lake itself for some more fishing till lunchtime. The afternoon/evening session would be at the Forbes Sagar.

There would be an occasional Mahseer, some Catla, Rohu or Mrigal. One would see the resident crocodiles and a school of otters. Once, I was lucky to see about a dozen, foot-long crocodile hatchlings swimming about, apart from the water birds.

We had ground baited an area where Sandeep had had good fishing for some time now, and soon, we had three rods cast out. The tricky part of the chosen spot was that we had to park ourselves on the bund road, as there was a steep slope of about 10–12 feet running from the road to the water's edge. Hooking a fish was easier than landing the fish. The ghillie would have to scamper down with the landing net, get a proper foothold and then land the fish while the angler waited higher up on the road.

The chosen spot had a large bed of water hyacinth close by, which apparently was a favourite feeding ground for the substantial population of Tilapias of the lake, and they too caused a lot of disturbance.

About a quarter of an hour had passed when I had my first bite. The fish had a good first run, but the 15 lb line was too heavy for the 11 lb Mrigal, which was quickly landed, photographed and released. The next fish picked up the bait and made a run for the bed of water hyacinth for cover. From the road, I could not get the proper angle to stop the fish, and the height from where I was fighting the fish posed an additional challenge to keep it clear of the hyacinth bed. However, despite my best efforts, the line disappeared under the hyacinth bed. I dropped the rod as low as I could and gently played the fish. After a considerable amount of time, I could cajole the fish into open water, and soon, I was holding a 20+ lb Catla. So engrossed was I in landing the fish that I had failed to notice that a crowd had gathered to watch the landing of the fish, and soon, to their collective surprise, the fish was released, giving rise to animated discussion, which I could not fully comprehend but enjoyed nonetheless. While all this was going on, Sandeep's main line came back without the feeder rig. The braid line had been cut, and we had lost the rig. The spare rod with monofilament line was rigged up and cast. After a while, I had a bite, and although the fish did not feel too heavy, the 'retrieve' felt strange, and soon, I found out the reason; the rig, which Sandeep had lost, was picked up by a Rohu of about 5 lb, which then had got snagged in my line. So, the feeder rig was not lost, and the Rohu was released safe and sound. Now, the spectators had seen it all.

Soon, the crowd dispersed, as the sun was about to set, and obviously they had to get to their destinations. The birds were on their perches to rest for the night. The fierce daytime sun was now a mellow red ball that soon disappeared. The trees were mere silhouettes that were standing guard for the night. Stars were beginning to appear one by one. At around 7.00 pm, I had another strike, and this time, it was a 20+ lb Rohu. In semi-darkness, the fish put up a gallant fight. Our ghillie had a tough time making his way down the hazardous slope with the landing net to land the fish. By the time the fish was safely in the net, unhooked and released, it was fairly dark so we decided to call it a day; but it was one of those days! While the rods were being taken out, the only rod in the water had a take. I asked the ghillie to wait near the water's edge, and soon, he had a 10 lb Mrigal in his landing net. What a fantastic evening of fishing!

# CHAPTER 11

The couple from Greece

I had the pleasure of hosting our first guests from Greece, Sakis Papantoniou and his wife Tsapi Vasiliki, who came over for a 10-day expedition trip for that elusive giant Himalayan Catfish – the Goonch, and if possible, the Himalayan Golden Mahseer.

Back and forth mails, advice on tackle, weather and what to expect on this tour was on for close to 8 months. Finally, we were picking up Sakis and his wife at 6.00 am from the Delhi International Airport.

Despite a 22-hour flight, the couple was ready for another eight-hour road trip. Soon, we were driving out of a still-sleeping Delhi. A short breakfast pit stop, where the couple was adventurous enough to sample South Indian idli-vada, sāmbhar/chutney with relish, we were off again.

Lunch, this time typical north Indian fare of dal, roti, subzi, dahi and then we were driving past Corbett National Park. Night halt was at a small beautiful resort on the banks of the Ramganga. An early dinner and the guests finally had a bed to crash on.

Next morning, after an early breakfast and a couple of hours of driving through the picturesque Ramganga Valley, Sakis and Tsapi were soon making their way down on horses. The group evoked a lot of excitement amongst children whenever they passed through small hamlets and villages. After about a couple of hours, the last part of the novel journey – crossing the Ramganga River on horseback and soon they were being welcomed at the camp, set up for the trip.

After stretching their limbs and cooling down with some chilled drinks, yes ice was regularly obtained, lunch was served. After lunch, the rods were made ready, and soon, the lines were being cast. As soon as the first rod was cast, unbelievably, the line started going out. Despite about two metres of line having gone out, the strike yielded no hook up. The waiting game had begun. The blazing sun soon turned mellow, the sky turned inky blue, and one by one the stars began to appear.

A cool breeze soon forced some thicker 'outerwear' to be pulled out.

The temporary shed erected with dried branches and self-inflatable mattresses on the sandy beach provided a somewhat bearable sleeping arrangement for whoever had to 'stand' guard. Bite alarms were activated after dinner and then began the night vigil. The rods, dear reader, never came out except for changing the bait, for the rest of the trip.

The night went by quickly. The Goonch lived up to their reputation – ELUSIVE.

Breakfast of baked beans, fried eggs and toast and fruit juice was most welcome. Sakis had got some excellent Greek coffee; the Turkish coffee evolved from that, the expert espoused. All in all, a great beginning to what really was the first day of fishing.

Soon local boys started appearing with their loop lines and nets, and natural curiosity drew them to the visitors. The locals are very much used to anglers next to the river, and soon they were back with foot-long Rock Carps (Goonch's favourite food), trapped in their loop lines, to earn a quick buck.

The day was slow except for Sakis getting a few Golden Mahseers, spinning from the rapids and some light tackle fun with the spunky brats.

That night, the bite alarm sounded twice but again no hook up.

The second day went very much like the first except that it rained at night, turning the weather slightly chilly.

The first real action came on the fourth night when the bite alarm started beeping. By the time Sakis scrambled out of his sleeping bag, about 3–4 metres of the 80 lb monofilament line had gone out. Strike and soon Sakis was fighting the fish. The fish was trying to rush into the deep end where razor-sharp rocks would shred the line and set the fish free. It was a challenge, made more so by darkness, then the fish turned and tried to go downstream. Sakis fought that off, and after about half an hour, the tired fish and the happy angler were united.

The tail tied the giant, and with first light, we were capturing images of the two protagonists for posterity.

Although the three rods were out, the fish were shy, so Sakis was advised to go spinning downstream in some of the deeper pools over the next few days. Juvenile Goldens were hooked and landed, but the biggies were still elusive.

Meanwhile, Tsapi had some wonderful birding during her treks with the naturalist. She visited local villages, made friends with the girls and sampled local fare while Sakis stayed next to the river.

With the trip drawing to a close, the couple, together with one of the boys from the camp, went downriver with a spinning rod. The second cast, with a 2-inch rubber shad, revealed GOLD, literally. The 12 lb line was peeling off in a mad rush, the reel screaming and Sakis trying to stop the run. An epic battle was unfolding. The fish was strong. Big rocks were offering the fish more than a fighting chance to beat the angler, so Sakis had to change position frequently to avoid being snagged. The low water was a help and also a hindrance. The fish could take cover amongst the rocks but could not make long runs. The pool was fairly long, and the fight went on for a long time. Sakis would bring the fish in, inch by inch, and then a slight movement would spook the fish, and off she would go in a mad rush. Gradually, the runs were getting shorter and less intense. Finally a gorgeous 50+ lb Himalayan Golden Mahseer was cradled in the arms of a very happy and tired angler. Fish of a lifetime.

The next couple of days were uneventful but celebratory. A decent Goonch and a spectacular Golden Mahseer being the highlights of the trip.

After a visit to the local temple and the village school, the trip was coming to an end.

Finally, on the day of the departure, the horses were back, and soon the Greek couple were bidding farewell to the river and the valley they had fallen in love with.

# CHAPTER 12

Deep-sea fishing

As the plane started her descent, the turquoise blue reefs circling the islands gave a certain sense of exhilaration. I was finally there. The hectic pace of checking in excess baggage and a large rod tube does fray the nerves a tad bit.

The last bit remained, collecting the baggage intact.

Anyway, half an hour later, with all the luggage safely in the car, I was on my way to the guesthouse, my base for the next week.

The sky was cloudy, and the air was moist. As we were coming into land, the angry sea was not a very pleasant sight, but now driving down to the guesthouse, the swell did nothing to soothe the nerves.

Once at the guesthouse, after meeting old friends, having a beer, eating lunch and snoozing, the evening was spent getting the rods ready. Two popping rods, 1 jigging rod and 2 trolling rods were my weapons of choice.

It had rained through the night, but now in the morning, the rain had stopped. Our gear and supplies were being loaded on the boat while we finished breakfast, and by 8.00 am, we were ready to get a move on.

As the boat left the jetty and moved into the bay on her way to the open sea, I found even sitting was difficult, leave alone standing. We came out of the bay and turned left, heading north. I was completely unprepared for the strong gusts of wind that hit us.

Some thirty minutes later, we came to a spot where the breakers were foaming over submerged reef, about 50 odd metres away from the shore – our first popping spot. We could not get too close, as the wind kept pushing us towards the jagged rocks. Keeping both feet on the deck itself was a task, leave alone casting a 180 gm popper some distance. Anyway, the first few casts saw 'follows' but no hook ups. When the hook up did happen, the GT (Giant Trevally) nearly yanked the rod off my hand. Trying to fight a GT while just about managing to keep your balance, with line being pulled out with the drag 'full tight on,' trying to keep the fish away from the razor-sharp reefs is an experience in itself. Time stands still, the back aches, the arms feel weak, and pain loses its meaning. Even a 12–15 kg fish appears to be more than a handful.

We landed 4 fish in quick succession before moving on.

The next popping spot was a tiny island, which the gulls and terns had made their home. The rocks were lined with their droppings. The sea was relatively calmer on the leeward side, and the water seemed deep and mysterious. It was stunning. I lost a fish in the first cast; the barbless hook was spat out as soon as the fish felt it. We landed a couple of brats, and then everything was silent.

By now the arms, shoulders and back were screaming for rest, so we set up the trolling rods and sat back.

Sitting or standing on the boat in rough seas is in itself a task. A passing shower added to the discomfiture, but soon a few spots of blue appeared overhead, and the sun made a brief appearance. The sea breeze and the sun helped dry the clothes somewhat. The islands in the distance made their appearances one by one, and suddenly, the tiredness was all but gone. The gulls and terns kept on flying out but could not locate any bait school to feed on. These birds help us locate a school of baitfish on the sea surface, which also attracts predatory fish. Once such bird activity is spotted, then casting into the bait school often results in bigger fish hook ups.

We selected a relatively shaded spot in a bay, away from the gusty open sea and had our lunch. I hadn't realised how hungry I was. A mug of lukewarm coffee after lunch and we were off.

We trolled for the next hour or so and landed Tunas, a few Dorados, a Spanish Mac and a few GTs, when suddenly, one of the boys located some heavy bird activity in the distance. We quickly speeded up, and after about ten minutes or so, we were near a huge bait school. The birds were having a field day, feasting on this bonanza. While I was getting my heavy popping rod ready to cast, I was warned that we were nearly above a reef. I set the drag on the Stella 20000 as tight as I dared to. The PE10 line was sitting on the reel, as if anticipating an impending battle whose outcome wasn't too predictable. I pulled my gloves up, tightened the fastener and then cast out into the wind.

As soon as the popper hit the water, the biggest GT I have seen, hit the popper, a clean breach, completely out of the water. The line started peeling off, the heavy popping rod bent double, and one of the boat boys tried to tighten the drag further. The captain revved the engines so that we stayed away from the reef and then I felt the coarse crunching of the line going through the reef. The fish was still diving when the line went slack. It was all over as suddenly as it had started. It was a gut-wrenching feeling, like a sucker punch to the solar plexus. But when you are in the midst of a feeding frenzy, there is no time for regrets.

One of the boat boys was casting my other popping rod, which suddenly started bucking like a wild bronco. When he handed over the rod to me, after setting the hook, line was still peeling off. I did not want to lose another fish, but it was the fish that was 'bullying' me. The fish dived, trying to get into the reef, and then went underneath the boat making me scurry to the other side. The boys figured out that we had hooked a Barracuda, and I was afraid that the fish, with its deadly dentures, would shred my fluorocarbon shock leader. About 10 minutes later, although it appeared close to an hour, the fish was in the boat. A beautiful animal. After a few 'trophy' photographs, the fish was released. The collective mood in the boat was still sombre, having lost the GT earlier. The collective consensus put the size to about five feet. Readers will appreciate that at that stage, or even now, the size was irrelevant. What we all agreed upon was that it was a monster fish. By this time, the bait school had moved away. The birds had more or less vanished, and there was a relative calm.

We were all tired and decided to head back. But there were still a couple of areas, which needed to be explored, so out came the trolling rods as we slowly moved along towards the harbour.

We had hardly gone a couple of minutes when one of the trolling rods started to bend over, and the reel started screaming with the line disappearing into the distant depth. As I removed the rod from the rod holder, I felt the fish, and she was heavy, very heavy. The heavy trolling rod had a huge trolling reel loaded with 80 lb mono, which was still peeling off furiously. In a while, the pace slackened, and I set the hook. The fish had dived, and now gaining line on her was going to be a herculean effort. Foot by foot, yard by yard, I fought her. Twice something spooked her, and she took off to greater depths. I lost more line than I had gained. The rough sea made the fight even more difficult. At times, the heavy swell tossed the boat around in a manner that made it seem like I was fighting an 'overhead' fish. The sun was setting. I got her near the boat, and the sight of the boat spooked her, and she dashed off again, line screaming. This happened a few times, but every subsequent run was shorter and shorter. I could feel her getting tired and so was I. My arms were like pulp; my knees had nearly lost the strength to hold me up. Whose strength would give up first?

In the gathering darkness, the fish came alongside the boat. I couldn't believe that the monster swimming alongside the boat was attached to my rod. As the tired fish swam alongside the boat, I felt a close sense of bonding with this magnificent animal. It was difficult to say who was more exhausted. A little while later, I would be back for a shower and a hot dinner while she will have to recover and go hunting for hers. The boys in the boat took over and landed the fish. I hardly had the strength to stand. The hook was removed, the fish was watered down and prepared for photographs. A little while later, when she swam away in the gathering darkness, it was the best sight ever.

Some thirty minutes later, we made our way to the jetty to berth our boat. Trudging back the half kilometre to the waiting hot coffee and shower, under the now starlit sky, I felt a complete sense of peace.

# CHAPTER 13

When we turned off the potholed road into the *kachcha* (unmetalled) road, it was already early evening. I have encountered small elephant herds on this road and was sincerely hoping that that would not be the case that evening, as I did not want to be held up in the dark forest for hours with elephants in the vicinity, who could be heard but not seen. Luckily, we reached the camp well in time for a quick bath and dinner. Sitting on the verandah with the river flowing less than 100 metres ahead under a clear starlit sky, the tiredness of the long flight followed by the drive from the airport soon drained off. One of the boys got us some coffee that I had asked for. We sat there chatting for a while and then returned to our tent.

The morning came all too quickly. We loaded our respective coracles and rowed downstream towards the head of the rapid. I tied the coracle some 100 metres short of the rapid and cast out. Soon I was reeling in a 15 lb fish. Vinay, on the far side, also had a few fish but nothing spectacular. The rest of the morning followed a similar pattern, and when the heat had become a little intense, we returned to camp. During the post-lunch session, I lost a huge fish. The take was spectacular, but soon I could feel the grating of the line and knew that it was being pulled through rocks before the shredded line was broken.

The next couple of days were uneventful – lots of fish but nothing big. It was still mid-November, and the water was high. The positive side, however, was that there were not too many anglers at camp. During peak season, the camp wore the look of a country fair, thus I always liked to get in and out before that happened. The fishing was peaceful and unhurried, just the way I enjoy it.

As softball ragi, hardball ragi and Chilwa was not attracting fish, I decided that a change of bait was warranted. There's a river that joins the main river some 4–5 kilometres downstream. This area was raided, and my ghillie returned one afternoon with a plastic bucket half-filled with crabs.

The next day, one of the rods was cast out with a crab. There was a stiff breeze blowing, and my cast was fouled up a bit and instead of landing in the main channel, I had cast my bait on the very edge of the tall grass growing on the side. After a discussion, it was decided to leave the bait there for some time, and if we did not get any bite, then it would be recast. The second rod with ragi was cast into the channel.

After about 20-odd minutes, the first rod started to show some life. A few knocks first, and then the tip bent. I allowed some line to go out, ensuring that the fish had the crab firmly in its mouth, and then I struck firmly. The fish took off like a mail train, turned left into the tall grass bed, and all went quiet. During the short run, I could make out that I had a biggie at the end of the line, and when all went quiet, I could not believe my luck. Two big fish were lost, and this had never happened to me earlier. As I tried to retrieve the line, I realised that not only had I lost a fish, but I was snagged too. We reeled in the other rod and rowed to where the line was snagged. As we tried to free the line, I felt some movement, and then some more. The fish was still on. The fish gave one big surge and broke free from the grass bed.

Having freed herself, the fish rushed off to the middle of the river, taking line and dragging us along.

There she went behind a crop of rocks that were slightly upstream. It was a tricky situation – one cannot row upstream in a fast flowing river, but the ghillies have handled such situations before. The coracle was jostled into a position on the farther side, and suddenly, the fish was in direct contact with the rod tip. Having blown her cover, the fish tried to go towards the other bank, but as I had a fairly tight drag, the fish ended up pulling the coracle, which made her tired. She still made us go through a merry dance in the middle of the river for well over a quarter of an hour. Gradually, she surfaced – massive tail and fins first – and then I could see her, thickset and huge. Having seen the coracle, she dove again. We were mid-river, and there was no way that we could 'land' her there and haul her into the coracle without damaging her or tipping the boat. We then decided to go downstream and land her on a sandy beach some 6–700 metres downstream.

By the time we reached the beach, the fish had recovered sufficiently, and another fight ensued. The fish dashed off downstream and took out line. As we had neared the beach, I had loosened the drag, expecting exactly this so the fish could take line out far more easily. It was another 15–20 minutes before we had the fish on the landing mat. I don't know who was more tired, the fish, the ghillie or the angler! And then the realisation dawned – I had not carried my camera. And lest the reader concludes so what, the cell phone camera is nearly as good, let me remind you that 1) the cell phone camera was not that advanced then and 2) as there was no cell phone signal available for miles, one did not carry their cell phones all the time. And then the kind lord took pity. I noticed another angler slightly upstream who actually was a world-class photographer. He was kind enough to take some great shots, which still allows me to relive those memories.

When I returned to camp, I got news that Vinay too had landed a 60 lb fish downstream in the afternoon.

# CHAPTER 14

We reached the small hamlet while the sun was about to set. The tiredness from the long drive seemed to melt away with the hot and sweet tea. It had rained sometime back, and the air was moist. It had been raining for the past few days, and I expected the river to be muddy. This was June-end, and the pre-monsoon showers were ushering in the rainy season.

Unpacking, a bath and a hot home-cooked meal for dinner made for a very pleasant evening. Art and Simon were softly urging me to be homeward bound, but I was already home.

We left for the river early next morning. Despite knowing what to expect, the sight of the river was a shock. Brown broth-like water, churning froth and debris floating past was a depressing sight, to say the least. But here we were, and we had the whole day in front of us.

I went upriver, spinning my entire collection of lures. Plugs, spoons, spinners were all presented at varying depths at various points over a stretch of about a kilometre but let alone a strike, I did not get even a follow. By the time I returned, the sun was up.

After a light breakfast, it was time to rig up the bait rods. The first rod was cast into a small rapid and the second rod further down towards the tail of the rapid. After about 30 odd minutes, the tip of the first rod shook violently, and about 15–20 inches of line went out before everything became quiet again. No hook up. By this time, the second rod had begun to twitch. The tip would bend a bit, and some line would go out, and then there would be a lull. This went on for some time, and I wasn't sure if it wasn't a Goonch (Himalayan Catfish) on my bait. Suddenly, the reel started singing, and after engaging the drag, I set the hook. Whatever it was, the end of the line felt heavy, very heavy. Then, just as suddenly, there was no movement. I was snagged! But it felt strange, the 'fish' would move a bit and would stop again. This went on for over 10 minutes.

Alam, my fishing partner, was convinced that it was a Goonch, and I was petrified that my 25 lb fluorocarbon leader would have been frayed by now and would snap anytime. Nonetheless, I kept up the pressure and gained line once in a while. My arms had begun to ache, and it was well past the half-hour mark since hook up. I would tighten the line up to breaking point and then suddenly open the bail arm – a tactic used to dislodge a sulking fish in the rapids. Repeating this a couple of times had the desired effect, and I gained line. Soon I was peering into the beady eyes of a huge soft-shelled turtle. Getting the turtle on its back took the two of us all our strength and guile before we could remove the hook with long-nosed pliers. As soon as we turned her around, she darted off into the murky water with amazing speed.

The rest of the morning was relatively quiet except for a 20 lb Golden on the first rod, which was in the rapid. By 1.00 pm, the rain came pelting down, and soon we were soaked to the skin. We decided to drive back to a dhaba we had passed on our way down and try and get a meal.

The universal one dish meal around these parts was rice and channa, which I never tire of eating. After lunch we had tea, and when the rain showed no signs of letting up, we called it a day.

The water condition was slightly different the next morning. There must not have been much rain in the upper part of the river, so the water condition was a tad better. We had the 2 bait rods out and were soon into fish. The first one was a feisty 20 pounder, and then we had 3 fish, all between 10–15 lb. The weather was muggy, and occasionally when the sun was out, it would beat down upon us mercilessly. We broke for a quick lunch and some shade and were back for the afternoon session. The afternoon was a bit of a washout except for a brat of about 10–12 lb. We had a long climb up the mountain path to the car and then a fairly long drive over the slushy dirt track due to the rains over the past few days.

There was no more rain, and the water had cleared some more by the next morning. We decided to bait up a third rod with some freshly caught Chilwa. In went the 3 rods, one by one, and then the wait began. It was unusually quiet for about an hour or so. We had some tea from our old faithful steel flask, pondering our next move, when the rod at the end of the rapid started to show some activity. The rod tip started to twitch, some line went out, and then it was quiet. The entire sequence was repeated a second time. I waited with the rod in my hand, and the drag engaged. When the line started going out a third time, despite the fighting drag,

I struck. The reel started singing. The first run nearly emptied my reel. I always fight my fish with a hard drag, yet this fish was unstoppable.

Looking down at my reel, I was worried. The metal base was showing, indicating that there was not much line left in the reel. The fish had by now reached the shallow run-off, and there she seemed to hesitate. I dropped the rod to my left and kept up the pressure, and she turned. She first swam up to the tail of the rapid and then went further left to the slack water on the other side of the rapid. By now, I had gained some line and was feeling more confident. The fish then made her first error; she got into the rapid and went upstream. Fighting the rapid soon tired her out but even then she turned once and then again and showed her massive tail and fin. She was trying every trick to spit the hook out, but I kept up the pressure and got her to the slack water on the near side. Although tired, it's never easy to bring in such a big fish. I was gaining line all the time till she saw us and made a mad dash for the rapid. The second run was a good 50–60 metres, but I ensured that the tight drag did not allow her to cross over and go to the other side of the rapid. She came in more easily this time, and although there were two more short runs, the fish was spent.

We soon had her on the landing mat and quickly unhooked her. The measuring tape was out, and she was an unbelievable 1.43 metres in length and 70 metres around her girth. Some quick photographs later, I held the fish facing upstream and allowed the river water in through her cavernous mouth and out through her gills. Soon, I could feel her strength returning. Releasing such a beauty is always a joy.

# CHAPTER 15

MARLIN on JIGGING ROD

The boat sped across the bay, leaving a foamy wake that melted into the blue sea. The April sun had already warmed the air. The two anglers were getting their popping rods ready, while the jigging rods quivered in the rod holders. The boat made a wide left turn, as they had spotted bird activity about a mile ahead.

As they neared the bait shoal, a group of dolphins swam alongside and then vanished as the boat slowed down. The sea was flat. As the two poppers flew to the middle of the bait school and hit the water, the reels started to sing. In about ten-odd minutes, two thrashing Tunas were landed, unhooked and released. In the next 15–20 minutes, four more Yellowfin Tunas, all around

12–15 kgs were hooked, landed and released. And then the bait school sank, and the sea was calm, mysterious, dark blue and enigmatic again. One of the anglers lit a cigarette as the boat moved further ahead. Soon the boat was slowing down again. The fish finder was showing some interesting graphics at around 150 feet depth. One of the jigging rods was lowered with a 250 gram purple and silver jig. In about a couple of minutes, the PE 6 rod bent over, and the fish was being pulled up, when suddenly, the line went slack. Before the angler realised what was happening, a 5 kg big-eyed Trevally flew out of the water about 30 metres behind the boat, followed by a Marlin, which was easily over a 100 kg. The Marlin splashed back into the water, turned around and hit the Trevally again. The Stella SW 10000 started to sing.

The first run was over 150 metres. The jigging rod was not built to handle this kind of a fight but withstood the first onslaught. The reel was loaded with PE6 braid, so there was still some line on the reel when the fish decided to dive.

The sea was calm, and the fight was going to be long and hard. The boat was being constantly repositioned so that the line was running clear. The angler was clearly getting tired, fighting this beauty on a light jigging rod. He handed over the rod to the second angler, who tightened the drag further, and inch by inch, foot by foot, started gaining line. He would gain about ten metres, and then the fish would take out another twenty metres. The sun was now overhead, and a light breeze was picking up. The fight had been going for nearly two hours, and while both the anglers were frayed, the fish was none the worse for the wear. By this time, the first angler had recovered enough to continue the fight.

Although gradual, it was still perceptible; the angle of the line was more obtuse now. The fish had come up and was at about ten metres below the surface and then suddenly the fish came up and jumped. Not once, not twice but thrice. The dark glistening form about fifty metres from the boat, tail walking and then splashing back into the dark blue water, managed to suddenly rejuvenate the anglers. The fight was now nearing its final outcome. The fish was now swimming at the surface, and everyone could only admire this magnificent animal. It was unbelievable that the fish was attached to this puny jigging rod, bent double, trying to exert some pressure to try and bring this gorgeous beast close enough for the others to haul him up and land him on the boat.

Another fifteen minutes later, two very tired but euphoric anglers along with two boat crew were hauling up this 110 kg black Marlin to be unhooked, photographed, revived and released into the beautiful waters of the Bay of Bengal.

# CHAPTER 16

It was still dark when we left Delhi on our way to Rishikesh. Somewhere after Ghaziabad, Google Map suggested a shorter route, but it turned out to be longer, time-wise. The scenic beauty adequately compensated for the bad road though. Sugarcane fields, canals and small villages dotted the countryside, but soon we were back on the highway. A couple of stops for breakfast and tea and then we were driving past Har-ki-Pauri at Haridwar.

Although it was only mid-September, the Ganga seemed very low. A short drive later, we were in Rishikesh. We met our guide, and he helped us check into a well-maintained guesthouse. Catching up since our last meeting followed after a late lunch, we exchanged notes on water conditions, latest catch reports and river stories. Next morning, we left at 6.00 am. It was a half an hour's drive to our destination for the day. The major highlight was when we went off-road to reach the river. A herd of about 50 buffaloes were wallowing in the slush outside the village and refused to take heed of us. With the help of the villagers, we were able to make our way to the riverfront.

The mighty Ganga flowed before us, powerful, wild, promising and intimidating.

Getting the tackle ready took a short time, and we were soon casting the lures and retrieving them. Strangely, the fish were shy – no hits, no follows. We went upriver, casting below the rapids, into eddies, but the result was no different. After about 2 hours of combing the stretch, we took a break and had our breakfast. Post breakfast, we put away our spinning rods and got out the bait rods. Some more time was spent in catching Chilwa, the baitfish. Even with bait fishing, all was quiet. The water level had risen considerably by then, the result of water being released from the Tehri Dam upstream.

Post lunch, the water level had dropped a bit, and then we started getting some action. The bait rods were out, and suddenly, we started getting bites. Soon, the first fish was landed, a brat of about 7 lb. More were to follow but all under 10 lb.

On the second day, we chose a different spot – a 2 km stretch of the river between two big rapids. The day followed a similar pattern – no hits or follows when lures were cast. Water started to rise and then receded, bait fishing picked up, but nothing happened on lures. We had some decent fish though. And the same thing happened on the third day too.

During one of our chats, I was told of the presence of The Golden Mahseer in a manmade lake/reservoir about 4 hours driving distance away. It was a temptation hard to resist for many reasons. I also wanted to see first-hand as to how the Tor Putitora was coping with the trauma of suddenly being confined to relatively still water from what was earlier a glacier-fed mighty river. Also, the water temperature would have changed, the feeding habit would have changed, pollution levels in a confined body would have gone up – all these factors would have affected this mighty fish.

So after 3 days of fishing the Ganga, we drove up to the lake.

After Rishikesh, the road suddenly improved, and we enjoyed the lovely drive. The only delay was due to a couple of chai halts, more to enjoy the surroundings than chai as such.

The first sight of the lake, from high above the water level, was spectacular. Post monsoon, the hills were covered with thick foliage. The water glistened in the early afternoon sun and was full of promise.

The place looked fairly deserted, with only a local market and some houses on one side of the road and a signboard of a water sport complex on the other side. A *kuccha* road led to a flat piece of land with a few tents, which I later found out, was the eating-place for the picnickers. A few motorboats and water scooters moored to the floating jetty completed the setting.

My first plan was to meet administrators of the water body, which I was told was the fisheries department located in a building close by. Asking for directions from some local boys, we made our way to a near-empty building and then to the section that housed the fisheries department. We were given the phone number of the boss who was located in the nearby town. She was very helpful, but as she was on leave, we were directed to seek the help of the local inspector. This gentleman was at his obnoxious best and told us to come the next afternoon despite explaining that all we were seeking was information regarding fish and their changing habitat and were really short on time. A few staff members, who were hanging around, informed us with great pride that Catla (Catla Catla) and Rohu (Labeo Rohita) fingerlings were introduced recently.

The next challenge was to find a place to stay, and after running around a bit, we were given permission to stay at the local guesthouse, a neat and clean place that was fairly well run.

Now for the main purpose – FISHING. The steep hillsides were a challenge, and we were told that the only way to cast a line was from a boat. We drove down to the picnic spot and negotiated with a local boatman to take us fishing.

It was already getting dark, so we decided to start early next morning and returned to the guesthouse.

At night, I was woken up by the incessant barking of dogs and found out next morning that a leopard, somewhere down the road, had killed a cow. This, after all, was leopard country.

We made our way to the jetty where our boatman met us, but as he had some religious function at home, he 'handed' us over to another boatman. The plan was to troll areas where streams and rivers joined the lake, and whichever location seemed promising, we would cast our lures and explore.

We let out two trolling lines as the boat was leaving the jetty and had an immediate take. It was a 4–5 lb Golden Mahseer that was reeled in and released. A good start to the day it was.

We trolled the far side and had two more fish, another 5 pounder and a larger 12 pounder. We tried plugs, spoons and spinners at various points but did not even get a follow. By now, it was around 10.00 am, and the air temperature was around 35° C but felt much hotter. We decided to return after lunch.

The afternoon session followed a similar pattern – we had 2 fish, trolling, both below 10 lb, but on return, decided to spin around the jetty. Despite the disturbance created by the water scooters, we had a 5 lb on a two-inch silver spoon. I was told that the locals used to catch a lot of the brat-sized Mahseer on atta paste, but now the fish were more wary and didn't take bait but would gobble up freebies offered.

We tried to spin with all kind of lures the next day, but again, no take, no follow. The boatman suggested that January was the best time for lures, as currently, the water level was too high, and the fish were scattered. But as the sun rose and the water warmed up, we had two fish on trolling, one being a respectable 30+ lb brilliantly coloured fish.

The afternoon session again yielded more fish of 2–5 lb. The Mahaseer were breeding in the lake, which is always a healthy sign.

The last day was windy, and it wasn't safe to be out on the open lake, so we trolled the creeks but drew a blank. We had a couple of fish spinning from the jetty. All fish were released.